GW00566911

A GAP
IN THE CLOUDS

A NEW TRANSLATION OF THE
OGURA HYAKUNIN ISSHU

First published in 2021 by
The Dedalus Press
13 Moyclare Road
Baldoyle
Dublin D13 K1C2
Ireland

www.dedaluspress.com

Introduction copyright James Hadley & Nell Regan, 2021
Translations copyright James Hadley & Nell Regan, 2021

ISBN 978 1 910251 82 9 (paperback)
ISBN 978 1 910251 83 6 (hardback)

Typesetting & Design: Pat Boran
Printed in Ireland by Print Dynamics

Cover image from a print by Utagawa Hiroshige (1797–
1858) showing Izu mountains with Mount Fuji in the
background. © BernardAllum / iStockPhoto.com.

The Dedalus Press receives financial assistance from
The Arts Council / An Chomhairle Ealaíon.

Aug 21
Dear Margaret –
lovely to meet
in the
Japanese
gdns
in
Cabinteely !

A GAP
IN THE CLOUDS

A NEW TRANSLATION OF THE
OGURA HYAKUNIN ISSHU

TRANSLATED,
WITH AN INTRODUCTION, BY

JAMES HADLEY
AND
NELL REGAN

Nell
Regan

DEDALUS PRESS

for Sarah Smyth

INTRODUCTION

⟐

OGURA'S 100 POEMS BY 100 POETS or the Ogura Hyakunin Isshu, is one of the most important collections of poetry in Japan. Compiled around 1235 by Fujiwara no Teika, its poems date from the 800s onwards and its poets include emperors and empresses, courtiers and high priests, ladies-in-waiting and soldier-calligraphers. Poetry was central to life and reputation among the ruling elite of medieval Japan, but these beautiful poems have endured because their themes are universal and readily understood by contemporary readers. They include love, loneliness and mortality, as well as the passage of the seasons and the beauty of natural phenomena. Many are steeped in the rites and sensibilities of the Shinto religion, with gods to be found in every natural thing. Over a fifth of the poems are written by women, among them, the famous poets, Ono No Komachi and Murasaki Shikibu, author of another classic, The Tale of Genji.

It is hard to overstate the importance of the Ogura Hyakunin Isshu in Japanese culture, up to the present day. Not only is it one of the most quoted books in Japanese literature, but over the centuries it was regularly illustrated by leading woodblock print artists, including Hokusai. It is still part of the Japanese national curriculum and has appeared in manga and anime films. In the early 20th century the Ogura Hyakunin Isshu was even turned into a popular New Year's card game called Uta-garuta, a kind of poetic snap, which continues to be popular in homes and tournaments across Japan.

TANKA — SHORT POEMS

The language of the poems is classical and highly condensed. Each consists of 31 morae (comparable to the syllable in English) arranged in the order 5, 7, 5, 7, 7. This form, the waka or tanka, will be recognisable to anyone familiar with the haiku, its younger and even shorter cousin. The tanka can be thought of as a poetic photograph that captures a scene in a single moment in time, but distils phenomena or situations that have taken a long time to come about. The poem itself zooms in on what can be seen at a single glance, often coupled with the viewer's emotional reaction.

As Japanese is replete with homophones, words with different meanings that sound the same, each poem is deeply complex and can often be read in two or more different ways, despite its brevity. The poets make full use of pivot words or kakekotoba which are tricky to translate into English. Exceptions include words like matsu – 'pine tree' and 'to await', often used in poetry as a synonym for 'to pine'. So it turns out that in the layered petals of Nara's cherry blossoms there is an allusion to the abandoned palace's intricate architecture (poem/page 61); that the character for furi can mean to 'rain down' and 'to age' (96); that sanekazura refers to a type of vine but can also mean 'to sleep with' (25) and that the playful waves of Takashi beach are also a covert invitation to adultery (72). Because of the nature of the kanji, one of the two calligraphic alphabets of the original, some of the poems also contain visual puns. Poem 22 is based around the fact that the character for 'tempest' is simply the character for 'mountain' on top of that for 'wind'.

Place names and natural phenomena are another signifier or shorthand with great resonance throughout the collection. A place name might simply be mentioned, leaving the reader to infer its relation to the rest of the line or block. Examples include Tatsuta River, whose banks are still renowned for their autumn leaves, the Ōsaka Gate, which in ancient times symbolised the barrier between the known world and a great unknown beyond, and Naniwa lagoon, once a major port whose tidal flats were dense with reeds. Natural phenomena are used in a similar way, and while a reader in English might readily understand that cherry blossoms are synonymous with spring and maple trees with autumn, it is a bigger leap to infer that mere mention of ariake, 'the waning moon of the second half of the lunar cycle, visible at daybreak', indicates a sleepless night! Daybreak and this specific dawn moon were deeply significant in love poetry of the time, not least because the aristocratic poet-lovers often lived in separate homes and had to part in the morning.

Bearing in mind all of these cultural references, the structure and music of the originals, as well as the grammatical structure of Japanese, decisions about what to carry over into new poems in English were at the heart of our translation process.

TRANSLATION

We, a translator of Japanese and a poet with no knowledge of Japanese, met fortnightly for a little over a year to work on the collection. To get under the skin of each poem, we sank into the kakekotoba and researched everything from the ancient practice of extracting salt from seaweed to the significance of wet kimono sleeves; from Shinto rituals to the exact white of snow falling on Mount Fuji.

What we saw as most essential to carry over in each translation was its immediacy, the emotional sting or tang at the heart of each drama, as well as its brevity and elegance. Many of the poems are about love and relationships and although the cultural context was crucial (for example, self-pity was seen as an erotic quality at the time) much of what is expressed is timeless. There are myriad interpretations, backstories, glosses, analyses and translations for each poem, but as much as possible we focused on the original text, puzzling out the physicality of its imagery. How exactly are autumn leaves 'building a dam' on a stream in 32, or making brocade on the Tatsuta river in 69? How is the poet, rowing out to sea in 76, mistaking a wave on the horizon for a cloud? Where is the poet in 51 as she waits in vain for her lover, and what burning herb is she is comparing her desire to?

As classical Japanese seldom uses pronouns, choices also had to be made about who was speaking in the poem and who was being addressed. Did the poet in 91 spend a night alone on a chill mat with only his own kimono sleeve for a pillow (I, my sleeve) or was it his lover/ ex-lover (you, your sleeve) or was he writing a third person narrative (he/she, his/her sleeve)? Mostly we decided to use the first person to achieve an immediacy and directness of address.

Direct or rhetorical questions are often used in these versions, as a way of evoking some of the compression and subtlety that results from another linguistic feature of the originals. In Japanese, many nuances of meaning can be expressed through grammatical particles, short words added on to phrases to indicate feelings like 'I wonder', 'I hope' or I'm sure'. One phrase can include many of these, resulting in brief, highly nuanced sentences, laden with conflicting emotions. In English these quickly become longwinded and clumsy, almost baroque. For example, 19 might read, 'Would you maybe say it must really have been no longer than [...]'. As these linguistic particles are frequently at the end of a 'line' or block they also serve to move the poem forward, drawing the reader's eye on from one line/image to another. This enjambment, where a sentence runs over a line break, is echoed in some of these translations.

In term of form, no attempt was made to replicate the pattern of 5, 7, 5, 7, 7 morae in syllables, but we did decide to keep to 5 lines throughout. This seems to allow for the tension and open-ended nature of the originals to come through. Couplets or quatrains in English can feel too settled or 'complete' to suit the open and suggestive nature of the Japanese aesthetic, where the image is allowed to do much of the work.

The acoustic patterning of the originals is powerful, and the poems are traditionally performed or intoned in a drone-like fashion. Some of this intricate vowel music is echoed in these versions, but only to the extent that it works in English.

Finally, as we gave primacy to the emotional heart or drama in each poem, we had to sacrifice or dilute some of the cultural references that do not immediately resonate in English, and that would distract from the new poem. So, for example, after many debates and drafts we took out the nusa in 24, the wooden wands used for purification in Shinto rituals; and the ajirogi in 64, the stakes of the wicker fish traps used to catch whitebait on the River Uji.

Along with the very brief biographies of each of the 100 poets at the end of this collection, we have provided notes for several of the poems where they might be needed or might add to a reading of it. However there is also further detail about the poems, a wider context and description of the translation process, as well as discussion about the titles of the poets available to download at *www.dedaluspress.com.*

Translation could be described as an act of love and patience. It feels odd, or perhaps apt, to be finishing this book during a pandemic, with all its attendant restrictions. The situation seems to magnify the sensibility of the poems, written in such a different place and time, which are all about paying close attention to the detail of one's surroundings, often from a place of isolation. Then, through a gap in the clouds, sudden illumination. At a time when many of us are rediscovering the beauty and melancholy of the natural world, it seems as though these brief but potent expressions of human feeling have not dated, not even after a thousand years

— JH & NR

OGURA'S
100 POEMS
BY
100 POETS

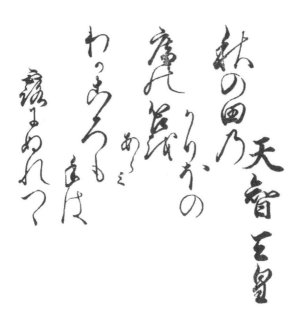

Autumn's rice harvest
       is on. I shelter in a lean-to,
its thatch so loose
       my sleeves
pattern with dew.

— EMPEROR TENJI

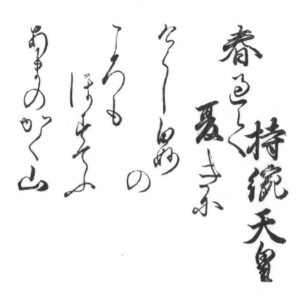

Our white robes air
　　　on the scented slopes
of Mount Kagu. Spring has
　　　passed it seems –
Summer is radiant.

— EMPRESS JITŌ

Alone I must sleep,
        I suppose. Night goes on –
long as the trail
        of a pheasant tail
through lily-of-the-valley.

— KAKINOMOTO NO HITOMARU

3

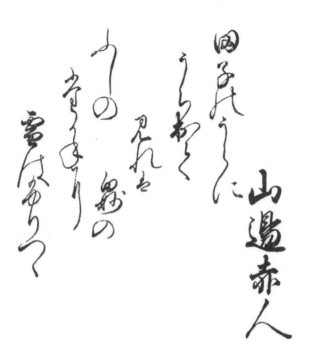

As I leave home
        for Tago shore –
such brilliance!
        Snow falling,
white, on Fuji.

— YAMABE NO AKAHITO

Deep in the hills,
    scuffing through
red leaves, I hear
    a deer cry out.
O the sorrow of Autumn!

— SARUMARU DAYŪ

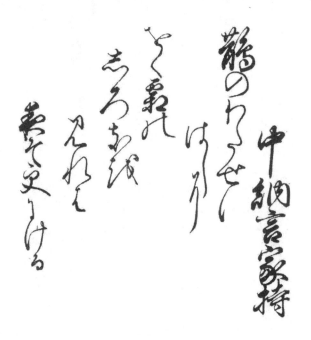

かささぎの
わたせるはしに
おく霜の
しろきをみれば
夜ぞふけける

中納言家持

I cross toward
        the sky
on Magpie Bridge.
        In white star-bursts
of frost, evening deepens.

— YAKAMOCHI
Middle Councillor

6

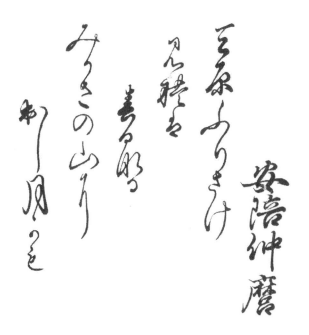

This moon I see
      as I gaze at the sky's
wide expanse
      must have risen over Kasuga
and Mount Mikasa too.

— ABE NO NAKAMARO

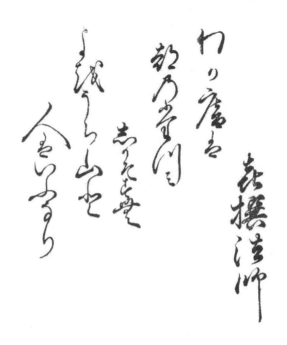

Such a life they think
       I live! As if my retreat
on Mount Uji,
       south east of this city,
could shelter me from grief.

— KISEN
Buddhist Master

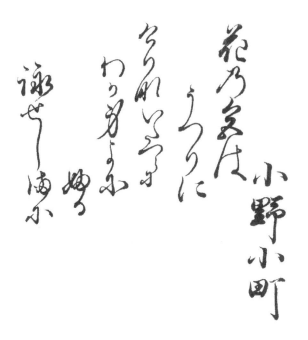

What use your bright
     petals now? They fade
in this endless rain
     just ... as I have,
gazing out at this life.

       — ONO NO KOMACHI

Here! This is the threshold of
    exile but also return,
of separation and encounter
    for friend but also for stranger.
This is Ōsaka Gate.

— SEMIMARU

The fishermen salute
        as they row out –
bound for the sea's
        wide expanse,
its scatter of islands.

— [ONO NO] TAKAMURA
Associate Councillor

11

Sky winds! Blow shut
        the route through clouds
so this mirage,
        these celestial beings,
might linger a while.

— HENJŌ
High Priest

12

The river – now male
      now female, bursts over
the ridge of Tsukube's
      peak, arousing
the deep pool below.

— EMPEROR YŌZEI

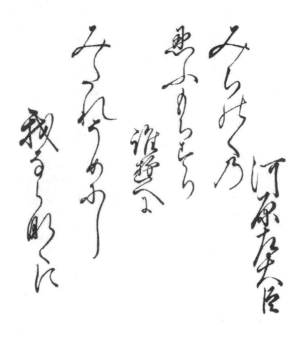

If not mine – then whose
      fault is it that my heart
is as crazed
      as the dyed patterns
of mojizuri cloth?

— KAWARA
Minister of the Left

I go out to the fields
        to pick Spring herbs
for you.
        Snow drifts
onto my sleeve.

— EMPEROR KŌKŌ

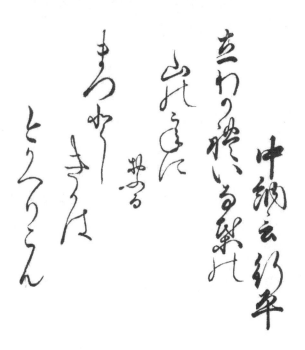

I go – will you wait
     like the pine that grows
on the peak of Mount Inaba?
     I'll send word of my return,
then hasten back.

— YUKIHIRA
Middle Councillor

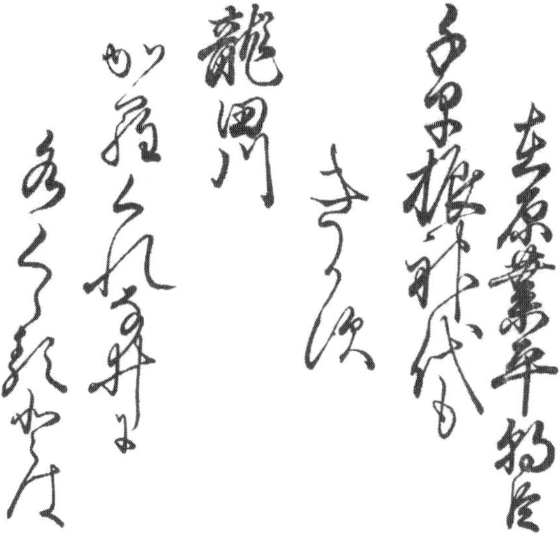

More brilliant and lithe
than past feats of the gods
is this sight –
Tatsuta's leaf-dyed
river, ablaze with red.

— ARIWARA NO NARIHIRA
Courtier

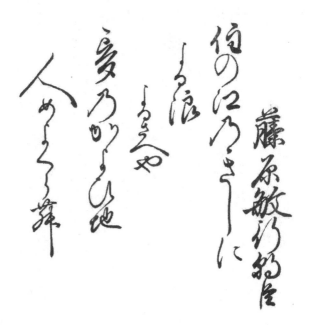

Evening tides rise
  at the mouth of Sumi River.
Why could I not sail, even
  through dreams, to be with you?
No one would see.

— FUJIWARA NO TOSHIYUKI
Courtier

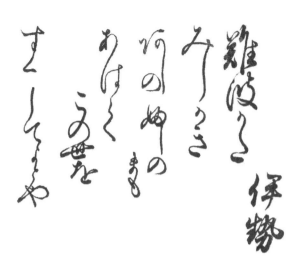

See the reeds of Naniwa lagoon,
  that brief span between
each notch – are you saying
  we've only been apart that long?
Already it's another world!

— LADY ISE

My anguish runs deep
    as the channels
of Naniwa lagoon. As
    my body breaks down – how
I long to meet you again!

— PRINCE MOTOYOSHI

You say you'll return
    soon so – I wait.
October's waning moon
    appears first
... then dawn.

— SOSEI
Buddhist Master

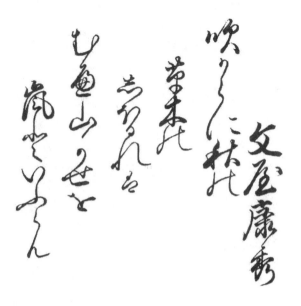

As gusts pick up, all
　　　Autumn's grasses and
her trees are blasted. Add
　　　wind to mountain –
it seems you have a tempest!

— FUN'YA NO YASUHIDE

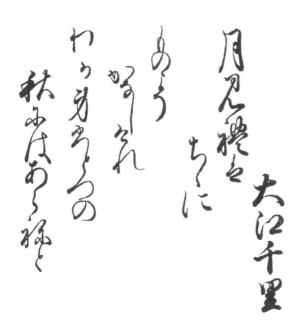

Sadly I gaze at the moon –
　　a million things flitting
through my mind;
　　Autumn has arrived
but not alone for me.

— ŌE NO CHISATO

This time – no time
       to make an offering
on Mount Tamuke.
       But look! At the shrine
the gods dazzle in red leaves.

— KANKE

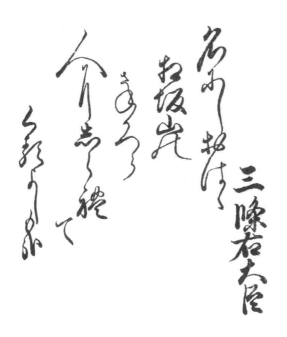

Like a tendril
    of the Ausakaya vine
I long to be entwined
    with you – and no one
would be any the wiser.

— [FUJIWARA] SANJŌ
    Minister of the Right

25

O maple leaves
    of the Ogura Pass –
if you have a heart, hold
    your fiery scatter
till the Emperor arrives.

— [FUJIWARA NO TADAHIRA]
Duke Teishin

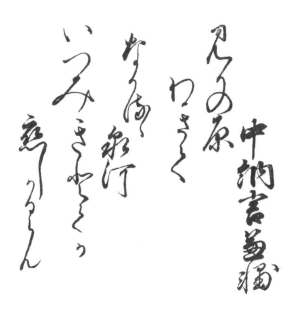

O such longing!
    The plains of Mika, split
apart by flooding springs,
    make me wonder – have
we ever been as one?

— [FUJIWARA NO] KANESUKE
Middle Councillor

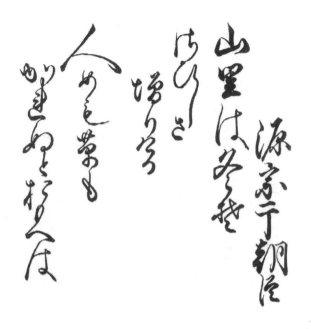

In this mountain village
      winter has the upper
hand. I watch as plants
      wither, people migrate –
only bleakness thrives.

        — MINAMOTO NO MUNEYUKI
               Courtier

Is this the white
       of the chrysanthemum
or first frost?
       My spirit thrills –
to pick or not?

          — ŌSHIKŌCHI NO MITSUNE

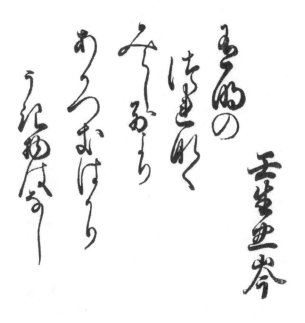

This waning moon
     is pitiless, as dawn
swiftly follows and we
     must separate –
such heartbreak!

        — MIBU NO TADAMINE

A faint light
        before dawn –
could it be the moon?
        Falling on Yoshino village –
white snow.

— SAKANOUE NO KORENORI

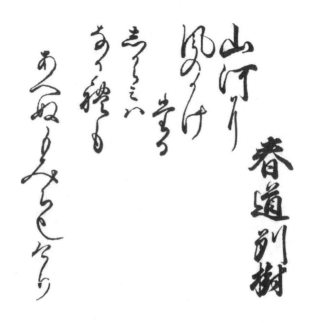

The wind builds a dam
    with maple leaves –
blown one-by-one
    they clog the flow
of this mountain stream.

— HARUMICHI NO TSURAKI

In the long light
      of Spring, my own heart
settles. I marvel at how
      petals fall –
such unrest.

— KI NO TOMONORI

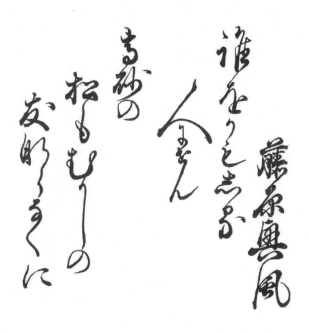

Is there anybody
        out there? I'm friendless
it seems – I can't even
        count on Takasago's
steadfast pines.

— FUJIWARA NO OKIKAZE

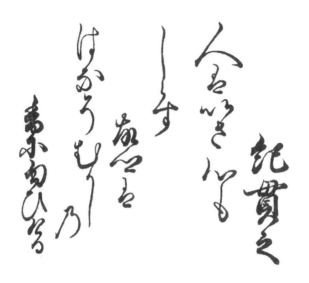

People's hearts I cannot
　　　read, but I know
the plum-blossom scent
　　　of my home town –
and how it endures.

— KI NO TSURAYUKI

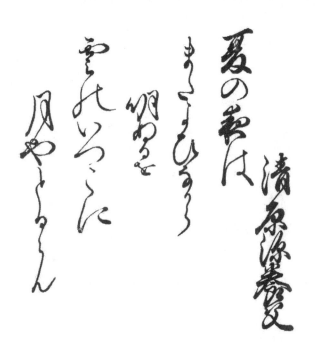

A summer evening, but
        such light!
The moon
        must have moved in
behind those clouds.

— KIYOHARA NO FUKAYABU

The wind tumbles
    white beads
of dew across
      Autumn fields –
a scattering of pearls.

— FUN'YA NO ASAYASU

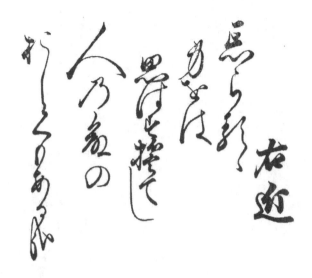

Forget when you go. Think
          not of me. But O it is
a disappointing thing; someone
          takes love's sacred vow –
then throws this life away.

— UKON

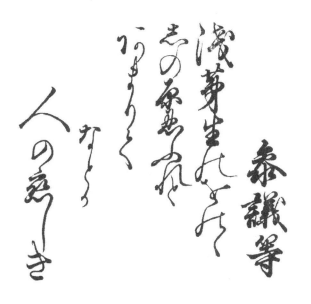

Like stubble in a field
        of bamboo, my feelings
are obscured –
        so why do I still
yearn for you?

— MINAMOTO NO HITOSHI

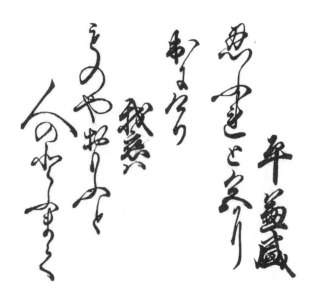

I try to mask
     my emotions,
but when asked
     who I love – I
cannot help but blush.

— TAIRA NO KANEMORI

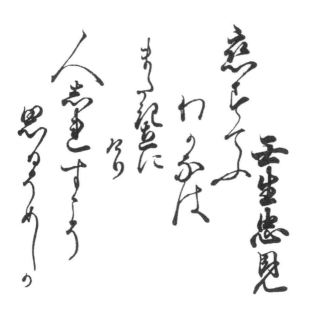

They say I am in love
     but I have only just
begun to feel it for myself –
     and so, I'd really prefer
if no one else knew!

— MIBU NO TADAMI

41

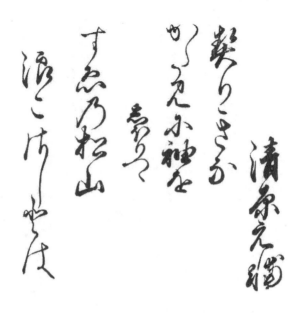

Betrothed! Our sleeves
    wring wet with each other's
tears – waves will breach
    this pine-tipped Mount
before our love will end.

— KIYOHARA NO MOTOSUKE

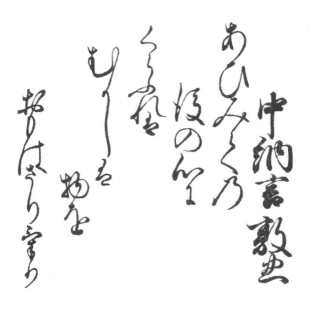

Blissed out
    after our rendezvous,
I realise that nothing
    my heart knew before
compares.

— [FUJIWARA NO] ATSUTADA
Acting Middle Counsellor

Is it circumstance or plain
       apathy …? Either way,
all hope we'll rendezvous
       wanes fast. Still, neither you
nor I will take umbrage.

— [FUJIWARA NO] ASATADA
Middle Councillor

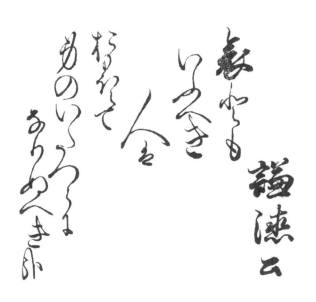

I cannot think
        of a loved one
to take pity on me –
        not one! It seems my
existence is futile.

[FUJIWARA NO KORETADA]
DUKE KENTOKU

45

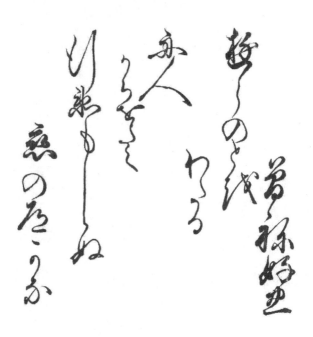

A boatman loses his oars
    at the mouth of the Yura –
he cannot know where
    he will end up. That's me –
caught in love's undertow

— SONE NO YOSHITADA

46

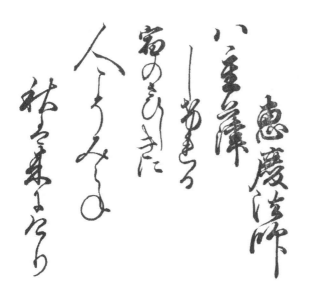

Vines take over
     the derelict house,
layer upon layer, a dense
     thickening. Not a person
in sight as Autumn comes by!

          — EGYŌ
        Buddhist Master

High winds, the waves
     are dashing the rocks! But,
battered by my own thoughts –
     I am the one
left broken.

         — MINAMOTO NO SHIGEYUKI

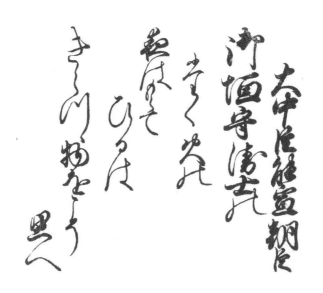

Like the lit braziers
        of the palace guards –
my thoughts of you
        blaze at night,
extinguish at dawn.

— ŌNAKATOMI NO YOSHINOBUASON
            Courtier

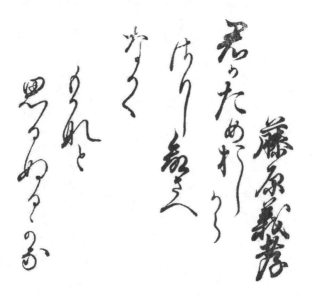

I thought
       losing my life
would be no great
       tragedy –
then we met!

— FUJIWARA NO YOSHITAKA

The thought of you – and I
    ignite like yellow mugwort
on Mount Ibuki.
    You do not know how
I burn for you – I cannot say.

— FUJIWARA NO SANEKATA
Courtier

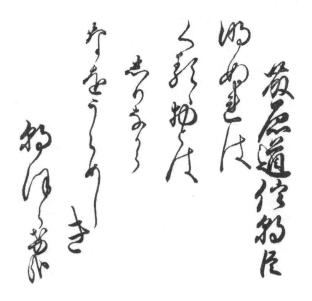

Knowing we must separate,
even though
the sun has barely risen,
makes of this
a bitter dawn.

— FUJIWARA MICHI'NOBU
Courtier

Nights I sleep alone –
   grieving
till the sky lightens.
      How much longer
will this go on?

— MOTHER OF IMPERIAL GUARD
            MICHITSUNA

To vow to remember
        till the end of time?
Too difficult and so I say –
        if my life ended today,
this would suffice.

— [TAKASHINANI KISHI]
        Mother of Gitōsanshi

The waterfall's sound
    died down long ago.
Even so, when its renown
    is invoked, I can hear it –
in full spate.

          — KINTŌ
      Senior Councillor

I am not long for this world –
    thoughts and memories
are one thing but
    I just want
to meet you again.

— IZUMI SHIKIBU

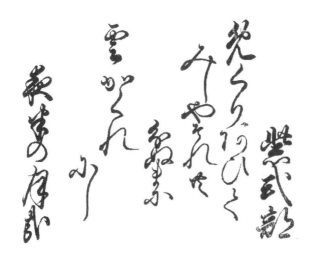

At first I don't recognise
        your face – we both travelled,
the years passed … then
        like a midnight moon once
hidden by cloud – I see you.

— MURASAKI SHIKIBU

How can I forget you?
        Each time wind stirs
in the bamboo grasses
        of Arima Mountain –
I yearn for you.

— DAINI NO SANMI

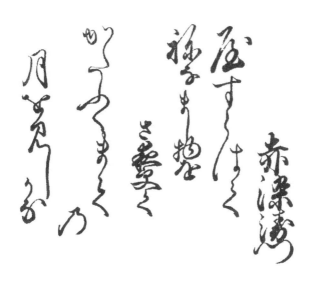

You must have nodded off ...
    I've been here, waiting
through the night.
    Now I see the moon set
behind western hills.

— AKAZOME EMON

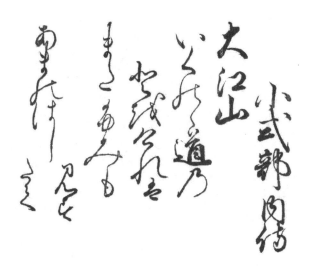

I have no leave yet
      to take the far road
to Ōe mountain and on
      to Amanohashidate, that sight
I've never seen. So I stay.

— SHIKIBU THE YOUNGER
    Maid of Honour

I view cherry blossoms
      in the ancient palace of Nara –
exquisite!
      Each double layer reveals
another inner sanctum.

— ISE
Undersecretary

So, that ruse might have
        worked in the classics, but
crowing like a cock
        as night wraps up won't
open these gates for you!

— SEI SHŌNAGON

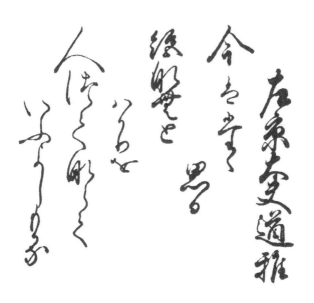

Is there a way
        to say that it's not just
gossip? Really, I have
        given up
thinking of you.

— SAKYŌ NO DAIBU MICHIMASA

Dawn and river mist
     on the Uji starts to clear.
Now, from its shallows,
     row after row
of fish traps appear.

— SADAYORI
Acting Middle Counsellor

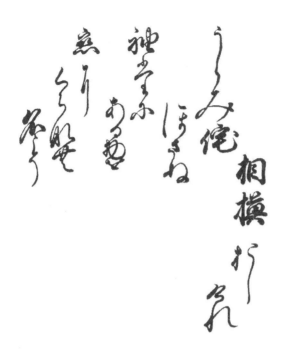

Oh how I resent
    that my sodden sleeves
have begun to rot. Such tears …
    Thanks to our 'love'
my name too is destroyed.

— SAGAMI

Other than you,
cherry blossom, my
mountain love –
there is no one
with whom I am intimate.

— GYŌSON
Former High Buddhist Priest

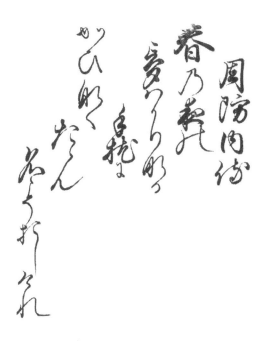

Spring nights are brief, even
     as you dream you wake.
Your arm pillows my head
     but should this end –
my name will be spent.

— SUŌ NO NAISHI

No matter how long
     I last in this sorrowing
world, the moon
     in the dead of night
will stay dear to me.

       — EMPEROR SANJŌ

68

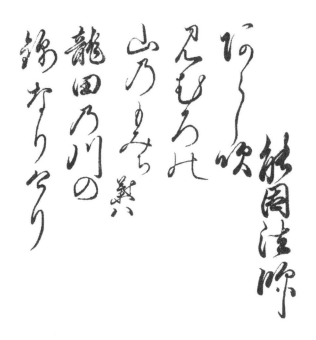

Maple leaves, blown
    by storms off Mount
Mimoro have settled
    on Tatsuta River.
Look – a red brocade!

               — NŌIN
          Buddhist Master

I leave my bleak cell
            to gaze about.
No point!
            Autumn twilight
is lonely everywhere ...

— RYŌZEN
Buddhist Master

Evening arrives,
    the leaves of the rice
plants rustle – through
    the thatch of my cabin
an Autumn wind gusts!

— [MINAMOTO NO] TSUNENOBU
Senior Councillor

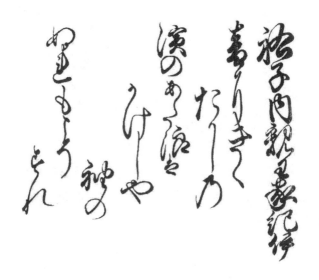

I ignore the flirtatious
    waves of Takahi beach
        as I do your advances –
    both would leave my sleeves
wet, in your case with tears.

— KI'I
Lady-in-Waiting to Princess Yūshi Naishin'nō

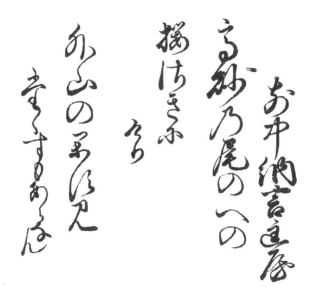

Cherry blossoms
    bloom on the high
peaks.
    O foothills, please
let your spring haze lift.

— MASAFUSA
Acting Middle Counsellor

Indifference abounds –
    I prayed at Hatsuseno
to the Bodhisattva of mercy
    but winter winds just
sent a bitter gale my way.

— MINAMOTO NO TOSHIYORI
Courtier

You promised, when I asked,
    that we would be blessed,
as dew freshens a herb. Look –
    it evaporates, another barren
Autumn has passed.

— FUJIWARA NO MOTOTOSHI

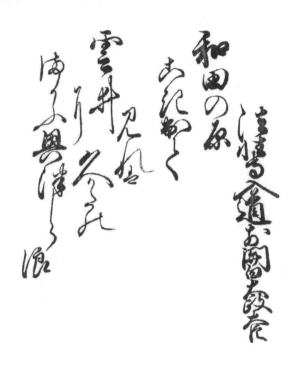

Rowing out on this ocean
　　　plain, I see a cloud
gather on the horizon.
　　　Not a cloud but a white
wave – the sea opens.

— HOSSHŌJI KANPAKU
Lay Buddhist Novice
and Chancellor of the Realm

A boulder blocks
     the river's quick shallows –
splits them
     apart. Surely
they must reunite?

— EMPEROR SUTOKU

The plovers' cries carry
        over Awaji Sound.
For nights now they
        have kept the guards
of Suma's Gates awake.

— MINAMOTO NO KANEMASA

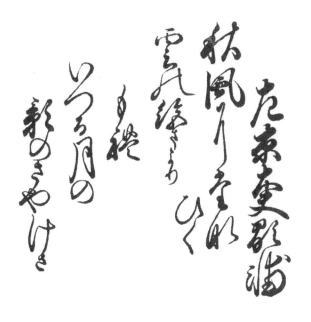

From a gap in the clouds,
    stretched thin
by Autumn wind,
    the moon radiates
its brilliance.

    — SAKYŌ NO DAIBU AKISUKE

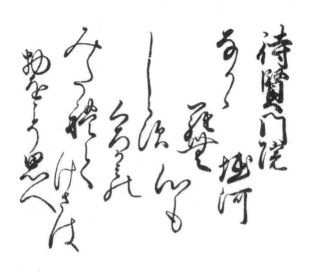

You swore to be steadfast
　　but this morning,
my black hair uncombed,
　　my thoughts tangled – I know
I don't know your heart.

— HORIKAWA
Lady in the Court
of Empress Dowager Taiken

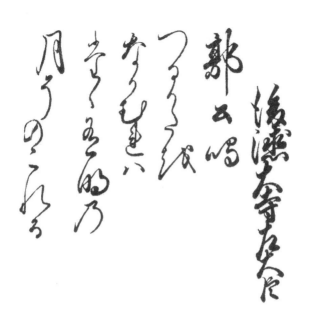

As I turn toward
　　　the cuckoo call –
only
　　　a dawn moon
remains.

　　　　　— GOTOKUDAIJI
　　　　　Minister of the Left

I will endure this life
     even though I fret
and shed tears
     of a grief that
cannot be borne.

— DŌIN
Buddhist Master

I am lost in thought
    about this world – our
inescapable state.
    Deep in the hills
a deer cries out.

— TOSHINARI
Private Secretary to the Empress

I may come to fondly
    recall this time, if
I live long enough.
    O bitter world,
I will love you – then!

— FUJIWARA NO KIYOSUKE
    Courtier

Night passes as I brood
        but nothing brightens –
even the screens
        of my chambers
are cold.

— SHUN'E
Buddhist Master

What is it about
     the moon
that says lament?
     Are my tears due
to the face it evokes?

          — SAIGYŌ
        Buddhist Master

A downpour! But
    before the pine leaves
dry, mist rises
    and Autumn dusk
descends.

          — JAKUREN
          Buddhist Master

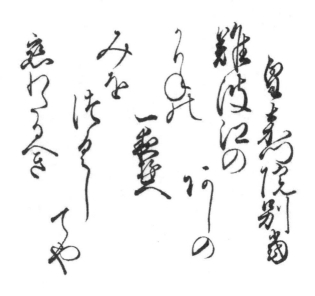

One night with you, short
        as Naniwa's stubbled reeds
and I am ... shipwrecked!
        Should I yearn for love,
fixed as tide posts in the bay?

— LADY-IN-WAITING
TO EMPRESS DOWAGER KŌKA

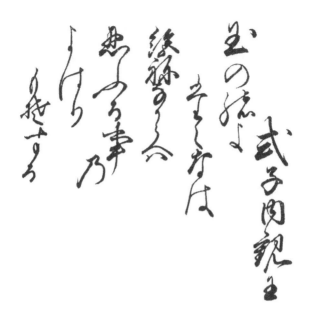

O my life's thread,
    if you are to snap then snap!
But if we are to go on then –
    bear patiently
until weakness is revealed.

— PRINCESS SHIKISHI

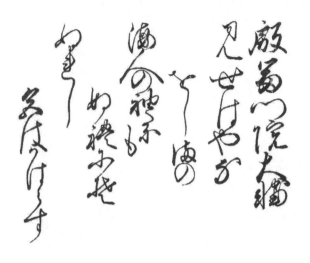

I want you to see the sleeves
     of the Oshima Island divers,
sodden over and over – still their
     colours stay fast. Mine stain
with my tears, turning to blood.

     — UNDERSECRETARY
     TO EMPRESS DOWAGER INPU

I lie on my chill mat,
    crickets call to the frosty night –
my only pillow the sleeve
    of my own kimono. It seems
I sleep alone tonight.

           — GOKYŌGOKU SESSHŌ
         Former Chancellor of the Realm

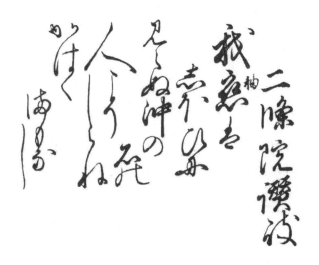

Like a stone in open sea,
        invisible, even at low tide,
my sleeves are submerged
        in tears – without even time
to dry. Still no one knows.

— SANUKI
Courtier to Emperor Nijō

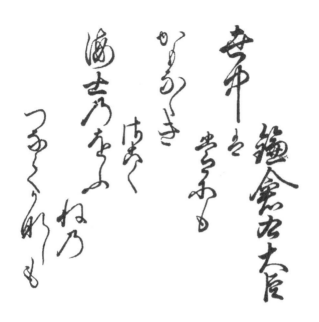

A fisherman rows
	at the waters' edge,
a rope towing his small
	craft. O, let this world always
remain so moving.

— [MINAMOTO NO SANETOMO]
KAMAKURA
Minister of the Right

93

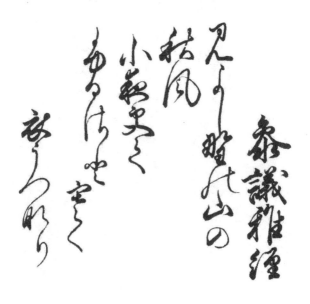

Yoshino in the dead of night –
　　　my sweet hometown chilled
by Autumn winds off the mountain.
　　　I hear the sound of women
at work, the beating of clothes.

— [ASUKAI] MASATSUNE
Associate Councillor

To enfold the manifold
  worries of the inhabitants
of our bitter world,
  I have come to the mountain
and donned a monk's black robe.

— JI'EN
Former High Priest

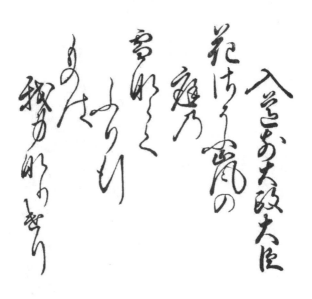

The storm passes through
and cherry blossoms
scatter like snow
on the garden – much as the years
shake loose as I age.

— [SAIONJI KINTSUNE]
Lay Buddhist Novice
Chancellor of the Realm

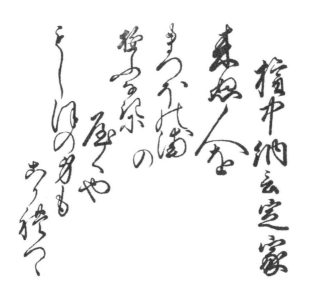

In the cool of the night
　　　I wait on Matsu'o beach
for you – like scorched
　　　seaweed salt I burn for you.
But you do not come.

— [FUJIWARA] SADAIE
Acting Middle Counsellor

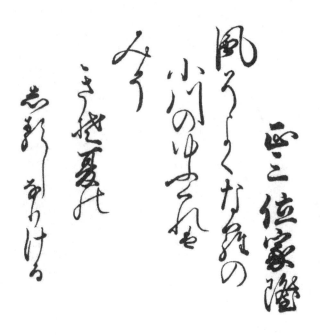

Dusk, a cool wind stirs
    the oaks on Mitarashi river.
At the shrine nearby
    the rites of Misogi are a sure
sign – Summer is not yet done.

        — [FUJIWARA NO IETAKA]
          JŪNI IETAKA

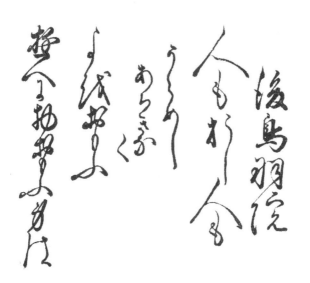

I am consumed
      by my own thoughts –
vexed with those I love
      and those I loathe.
This world has lost its zest.

— EMPEROR GO-TOBA

Ferns trail from
        the derelict eaves
of the Imperial Court –
        it's hard not to dwell
on the glory days …

— EMPEROR JUNTOKU

Biographies and Notes

The following abbreviations are used to identify the poets included in these canonical texts:
• The Rokkasen or Six Poetry Immortals – Immortal 6;
• Kintō's The Thirty-Six Immortals of Poetry – Kintō's 36;
• Norikone's The Late Classical Thirty-Six Immortals – Late Classical 36;
• The Thirty-Six Female Immortals of Poetry – Female 36.

1. Emperor Tenji (626 to 672), reigned from 661 to his death and is best known for strengthening central imperial control, and developing the first Japanese legal code. In the earlier eighth-century collection the Man'yōshū the same poem is attributed to Anonymous.

2. Empress Jitō (reigned 686–697), third of eight Empresses to rule in their own right who was daughter of the Emperor Tenji (poem 1). She married her uncle Emperor Tenmu, after whose death she ruled. Her poetry is also included in the Man'yōshū.
NOTE: The word shirotae (白妙), used here and in poem 4, originally meant a specific kind of pure white cloth made from the bark of the mulberry tree. In Japanese it has come to mean simply "white cloth" or "pure white".

3. Kakinomoto no Hitomaro (d.c. 707), classed as the first of the four greatest Japanese poets, the other three being Fujiwara no Teika (poem 97), Sōgi and Bashō. A variant of this poem appears in Man'yōshū under Anonymous. Immortal 6, Kintō's 36.

4. Yamabe no Akahito (c. 724–736), a court poet who often travelled with Emperor Shōmu (724–736). This poem is one of the earliest descriptions of Mt. Fuji. Kintō's 36.
NOTE: For shirotae (白妙), see poem 2.

5. Sarumaru Dayū (possibly late 8th C), there is no information extant about him – some believe him to have been Prince Yamashiro no Ōe. Kintō's 36.
NOTE: The word for deer, shika (鹿), used here and in poem 83 probably refers to the Sika deer, native to East Asia. It was often invoked for its autumn cry, a haunting whistle or high-pitched screech, very different from the roar of the Eurasian Red Deer stag.

6. Otomo no Yakamochi (c.718–785), the most prominent writer of his day and compiler of the Man'yōshū of which his own poetry comprised ten percent. A Middle Councillor, he was heavily involved in Court plots and posthumously disgraced because of these. Kintō's 36.
NOTE: The poem appears to reference a bridge in the Imperial Palace of the time. It was named after the classic legend in which star-crossed lovers, separated by the Milky Way, were reunited after magpies built them a bridge using their wings. Inspired by this legend, the Tanabata (七夕) Festival is celebrated in Japan on 7 July every year.

7. Abe no Nakamaro (710–790), a scholar and poet who moved to China and worked for the Tang court as governor of Annam (in present-day northern Vietnam). He was a close friend of leading Chinese poets Li Bai and Bao Xin. He was unable to return to Japan before his death.

8. Kisen (mid 9th C), a Buddhist Master and poet who lived in Ujiyama, south-east of Kyoto. Little else is known about him and this is one of only two poems attributable to him. Immortal 6

9. Ono no Komachi (mid 9th C), a legendary poet and the only woman in the Rokkasen or Six Poetry Immortals. She was the granddaughter of Ono no Takamura (poem 11) and had at least seven Nō plays written about her. Immortal 6, Kintō's 36.
NOTE: The word hana 花, used here and in poems 33, 35 and 96, literally means "flower", but is used poetically in Japanese, even today, to mean cherry blossom. There is one exception in this collection, which is poem 35, where the flowers are not cherry blossoms, but plum blossoms.

10. Semimaru (c. early/ mid-9th C), a hermit, legendary poet and blind lute player who lived on Ausaka. He was the subject of the Nō play Semimaru.
NOTE: The Ausaka Gate (pronounced Ōsaka, but not to be confused with the modern-day city) referenced in the poem was an important tollgate which was seen as a barrier between the known, 'civilised' capital and the unknown, outside world. It is located between the present-day Kyoto and Shiga prefectures.

11. Ono no Takamura (802–853), a leading poet and State Councillor who spent his career falling in and out of favour with the Emperor. He came from an illustrious family, and among his descendants was Ono no Komachi (poem 9).

12. Henjō or Yoshimine no Munesada (816–890), a powerful courtier who became a Buddhist Master and rose rapidly in the religious ranks. He was rumoured to have had a love affair with Ono no Komachi. Immortal 6, Kintō's 36

NOTE: This poem refers to the Feast of Light, when the first fruits of autumn were presented to the Emperor. The dancers, who were the daughters of courtiers, represented moon maidens only able to return home through cloudy skies.

13. Emperor Yōzei (869–949), the 57th Emperor of Japan, who ruled from the age of 8 to 15 but was forced to abdicate because of his cruel behaviour. He subsequently dedicated himself to poetry, but this is his only poem in any classical anthology.

14. Kawara no Sadaijin or Minimoto no Tōru (822–895) The son of Emperor Saga and reputed to be one of the models for the eponymous Genji in The Tale of Genji.
NOTE: Patterns on mojizuri (もぢずり) cloth were made by rubbing plant dye onto material laid over a stone. The method took its name from the area in which it was made, Shinobu (also mentioned in the Japanese).

15. Emperor Kōkō (830–887), the 58th Emperor who took over when Yōzei (poem 13) abdicated.
NOTE: The Spring herbs referred to are wakana, (若菜), seven young edible Spring greens traditionally made into a seasonal tonic. Gathering these was a social occasion for young courtiers at the time while a Wakana Shinji or ritual still takes place in Japan, every year on 7th January.

16. Ariwara no Yukihira (818–893), a Middle Counsellor and Governor of Inaba who was skilled in Chinese verse. He was half-brother of Ariwara no Narihara (poem 17), and may have been another model for the Genji character.

17. Ariwara no Narihra (825–88?), considered one of the best poets of his day, he was the grandson of two Emperors. Immortal 6, K36.

NOTE: Just as cherry blossom is synonymous with spring in Japanese culture, so red maple leaves are synonymous with autumn. The Tatsuta riverbank was renowned for its maple trees and the characters 紅葉 used to indicate the Japanese maple (momiji) individually mean "crimson" and "leaves". In the Japanese, the poet does not even have to specify that it is the leaves dying the river red.

See also Translators Note p. VII and poems 24, 26, 32, 69.

18. Fujiwara no Toshiyuki (d. 991), a renowned calligrapher as well as a poet and courtier who served as Emperor's captain of the guard. K36.

19. Lady Ise (c.873 –c.938), a Lady-in-Waiting and favourite of Emperor Uda, she subsequently had a child with his son Atsuyoshi. A total of 184 of her poems are in Imperial Anthologies. K36.

NOTE: There was a profusion of reeds (ashi 芦) growing in Naniwa Lagoon (near present-day Ōsaka city) when the poems were composed. The reference also appears in poems 71 and 88.

20. Prince Motoyoshi (890–943), the eldest son of Emperor Yōzei who was famous as a lover.

21. Sosei (mid 9th C), a Buddhist Master who was the son of Henjō (poem 12) and a renowned calligrapher. K36

NOTE: Several of the poems (30, 31, 81 as well as this one) mention ariake (有明) which translates as the waning moon of the second half of the lunar cycle, i.e. the 16th night on, when the moon is visible until dawn. It usually implies that the narrator has spent a sleepless night.

22. Fun'ya no Yasuhide (c. late 9th C.), became Court director of the wardrobe in 879, probably for poetic, rather than administrative prowess. Immortal 6.

NOTE: The Japanese poem actually incorporates a visual pun – the character for tempest (嵐) is composed of the character for mountain (山) on top of that for wind (風).

23. Ōe no Chisato (c. 889–923), a nephew of Ariwara no Yukihira (poem 16) and Ariwara no Narihira (poem 17), he was known for the Kudai Waka collection, based on Chinese poetry and ordered by Emperor Uda. He was later banished to the Iyo Province of Shikoku Island.

24. Kanke (845–903) or **Sugawara no Michizane**, a governor of Dazaifu, he wrote in Japanese and Chinese and was deified after his death. Known as Tenjin, the Shinto god of letters, students still pray to him before exams.

NOTE: The poem references a particular type of offering or ritual object – a nusa (幣), a wooden wand, decorated with long strips of paper, used for Shinto Buddhist purification rites.

25. Fujiwara no Sanjō or Sadakata (873–932), a Minister of the Right, he was the father of Atsutada (poem 44).

NOTE: In the Japanese the vine is a creeping variety called sanegazura (さねかづら) while sane (小寝) can also mean to sleep together.

26. Fujiwara no Tadahira (880–949), also Duke Teishin, a Grand Chancellor and grand minister.

NOTE: Apparently former Emperor Uda was so taken with the autumn leaves of Mount Ogura, that he ordered a poem be composed to encourage his heir, Emperor Daigo, to visit the area.

27. Fujiwara no Kanesuke (877–933), a Middle Councillor and cousin of Fujiwara no Sadakata (poem 25), as well as colleague of Mibu no Tsurayuki (poem 35) and Ōshikōchi no Mitsune (poem 29). Kintō's 36.

28. Minamoto no Muneyuki (d.939), a courtier and grandson of Emperor Kōkō (poem 15). Kintō's 36.

29. Ōshikōchi no Mitsune (d. 925), one of the compilers of the Kokinshū, the first Imperial poetry anthology and along with Ki no Tsurayuki, (poem 35), best represented in that anthology. Kintō's 36.

30. Mibu no Tadamine (b c.850) The father of Mibu no Tadami (poem 41) and another of the compilers of the Kokinshū.

31. Sakanoue no Korenori (late 9th–early 10th C), governor of Kaga Province, but he was better known as a champion of kemari, a classical Japanese version of football. Kintō's 36.

32. Harumichi no Tsuraki (d. 920), appointed governor of Oki Province but he died before he could take up his post.

33. Ki no Tomonori (d. c. 905), a cousin of Ki no Tsurayuki (poem 35) and a compiler of the Kokinshū. He died soon after it was finished. Kintō's 36.

34. Fujiwara no Okikaze (early 10th C), a well-known competitor in poetry challenges and a koto musician. Kintō's 36.
NOTE: Takasago in the Hyōgo Prefecture is renowned for its pine trees: needles cover the streets; the town mascot is a pinecone and one pair of pine trees found in the Shrine is a mythological symbol of love and marriage.

35. Ki no Tsurayuki (868 – 945), the chief compiler of the Kokinshū who was considered the greatest poet of his time. He campaigned to have Japanese poetry regarded as equal to Chinese. Kintō's 36.
NOTE: See poem 9.

36. Kiyohara no Fukayabu (early 10th C), grandfather of Kiyohara no Motosuke (poem 42) and the great grandfather of Sei Shōnagon (poem 62).

37. Fun'ya no Asayasu (late 9th–early 10th C), a son of Fun'ya no Yasuhide (poem 22) who took part in many poetry competitions.

38. Ukon (late 9th–early 10th C), a Lady-in-Waiting to Empress Consort Onshi and daughter of Fujiwara no Suenawa. She was known for her many love affairs some of which were related in Tales of Yamato.

39. Minamoto no Hitoshi (880–951), great-grandson of Emperor Saga, towards the end of his life he was appointed Sangi Counsellor of the Fourth Rank.
NOTE: The poem mentions asaji 〔浅茅〕, a sparsely growing cogon grass, often used in literature to evoke a bleak landscape.

40. Taira no Kanemori (d. 990), a governor of Suraga and descendent of Emperor Kōkō (poem 46). Kintō's 36.

41. Mibu no Tadami (early/mid 10th C), the son of Mibu no Tadamine (poem 30), he was also one of Kintō's Thirty-Six Immortals of Poetry. Kintō's 36.

42. Kiyohara no Motosuke (908–990), a governor of Higo Province on western Kyushu island, and attached to the Bureau of Poetry in 951. He was the grandson of Kiyohara no Fukayabu (poem 36) and father of Sei Shōnagon (poem 62) Kintō's 36.

NOTE: The long, hanging sleeves of a traditional kimono, (袖) were culturally very important and appear in many of the poems. Here as well as in poems 65, 72, 90 and 92 the phrase to 'wring the sleeves' is used. As people during this period wiped their tears on their sleeves, overwhelming grief was illustrated by how stained one's sleeves were. See also notes for poems 67, 91 and 95, where the mention of sleeves comes with very different connotations.

43. Fujiwara no Atsutada (906–943), an acting Middle Counsellor who was as renowned as a musician as he was for his love affairs, stories of which appeared in literature. Kintō's 36.

44. Fujiwara no Asatada (910–966), a Middle Councillor who was the son of Fujiwara no Sadakata (poem 25). Kintō's 36.

45. Fujiwara no Koretada also Duke Kentoku (924–972), a Regent and Grand Minister and Director of the Bureau of Poetry.

46. Sone no Yoshitada (late 10th C), a Secretary in Tango who was viewed as an eccentric by contemporary poets. By the 12th century he was being hailed as an innovator for the freshness and vitality of his poetry.

47. Egyō (late 10th C), a Buddhist Master and one of Fujiwara no Norikone's Late Classical Thirty-Six Immortals of Poetry. Late Classical 36.

48. Minamoto no Shigeyuki (died c.1000), went with Fujiwara no Sanekata (poem 51) when he took up his post as governor of Mutsu Province, on north-eastern Honshū Island. Kintō's 36.

49. Ōnakatomi no Yoshinobu (921–991), a courtier and member of the Bureau of Poetry. It is possible that this poem has been falsely attributed to him. Kintō's 36.

50. Fujiwara no Yoshitaka (954–974), a son of Fujiwara no Koretada (poem 45) who died young of smallpox. Late Classical 36.

51. Fujiwara no Sanekata (d.994), a courtier, governor of Mutsu Province on the north-east of Honshu island, and great grandson of Fujiwara no Tadahira (poem 26).
NOTE: This poem and poem 75 refer to sashimogusa (さしも草) and sasemo (させも) or Japanese mugwort, a herb found across East Asia and widely used in cooking and for moxibustion in traditional medicine.

52. Fujiwara Michinobu (971–994), a courtier who was apparently also a brilliant Commander of the Guard. He died at 23. Late Classical 36.

53. Mother of Imperial Guard Michitsuna (c. 935–995), true name unknown, a poet and author of Kagerō Nikki, a classic of Japanese literature, which concerned her troubled marriage. She was also known for her exceptional beauty. Late Classical 36.

54. Takashinani Kishi, Mother of Gitōanshi (d. 996), the wife of a Grand Chancellor, among her children was the Empress consort Teishi.

55. Fujiwara no Kintō (996–1041), a Senior Counsellor who subsequently entered the Buddhist clergy. He was a revered critic who compiled the first and most famous list of The Thirty-Six Immortals of Poetry.

56. Izumi Shikibu (977–c.978), considered the greatest of the many talented woman poets of the Heian period, she was a Lady-in-Waiting for Empress Shōshi along with Murasaki Shikibu (poem 57). She was also the mother of Shikibu the Younger (poem 60) Late Classical 36.

57. Murasaki Shikibu (c.978–c.1014), true name unknown, a prolific poet and novelist, best known for The Tale of Genji, widely considered to be the world's first novel. She was Lady-in-Waiting to Empress Shōshi. Late Classical 36.

58. Daini no Sanmi (b.c. 999), the daughter of Murasaki Shikibu (poem 57) and nurse to Emperor Go-Reizei. The last ten chapters of The Tale of Genji are sometimes attributed to her.
NOTE: During this period the area around Arima Mountain was covered in sasa (笹), the bamboo grass mentioned in the poem. It is a small, low-grown species, with multiple thin stems.

59. Akazome Emon (mid 10th C–mid-11th C), a poet and historian, she was Lady-in-Waiting to Empress Shōshi at the same time as Izumi Shikibu (poem 56) and Murasaki Shikibu (poem 57). She appears in Murasaki Shikibu's diary in an unflattering light. Late Classical 36.

60. Shikibu the Younger (d. 1025), a daughter of Izumi Shikibu (poem 56) she was also a Lady-in-Waiting to Empress Shōshi. She died in her 20s.

61. Ise no Taifu (early 11th C), granddaughter of Ōnakatomi no Yoshinobu (poem 49) and Lady-in-Waiting to Empress Shōshi. Late Classical 36.

62. Sei Shōnagon (c.965–c.1025), author of the classic The Pillow Book and one of the greatest of the Heian period's women writers. She was the daughter of Kiyohara no Motosuke (poem 42) and great-granddaughter of Kiyohara no Fukayabu (poem 36) Late Classical 36.
NOTE: A classical Chinese story is invoked in this poem. An army fleeing the King of Qin was stopped from leaving his territory at the Hangu Pass. The gates were to be closed until dawn but when a soldier mimicked a cock-crow, the real cockerels started crowing and the gates were opened. 'Passing through Ōsaka Gate' is in the original poem but in fact this was a common double entrendre alluding to couples sleeping together.

63. Sakyō no Daibu Michimasa or Fujiwara no Michimasa (992–1054), a violent man who displeased one Emperor after an affair with the former High-Priestess of the Ise Grand Shrine. Later the daughter of Emperor Kazan was murdered, apparently on his orders.

64. Fujiwara no Sadoyori (995–1045), an acting Middle Counsellor, renowned poet and calligrapher, he was the eldest son of Fujiwara no Kintō (poem 55) and grandson of Emperor Murakami. Shikibu the Younger's poem (60) was dedicated to him. Late Classical 36.
NOTE: The original refers to the ajirogi (網代木) which were traps used to catch small fish during wintertime. Stakes were driven into the riverbed in the shallows and a mat of thin woven bamboo or tree branches (kasu 簀) attached. They were a sight particularly associated with the Uji River.

65. Sagami (early 11ᵗʰ C), also known as Oto-jijū. Her husband was governor of Sagami (now Kanagawa) from where she took her nickname. Late Classical 36.
NOTE: See poem 42.

66. Gyōson (1055–1135), a former Buddhist High Priest who was a mountain hermit in the Shugendō or Japanese folk religion tradition. He also established pilgrim routes and became leader of the Tendai sect.

67. Suō no Naishi (d.c. 1110), the daughter of the governor of Suō Province on the eastern end of Honshu island, and a handmaiden to four Emperors she became a Buddhist nun just before she died.
NOTE: During the Heian period, lovers would use the sleeves (sode 袖) of one another's kimono as pillows. Poem 91 also refers to this.

68. Emperor Sanjō (976–1017), the 67ᵗʰ Emperor of Japan, who reigned from 1011 to 1016. After abdicating in favour of his cousin, he entered a Buddhist monastery and died soon after.

69. Nōin (988–1051), a Buddhist Master who studied Chinese literature before entering religious life. He wrote a famous treatise on poetry, the Nōin Utamakura. Late Classical 36.
NOTE: See poem 17.

70. Ryōzen (early 11ᵗʰ C), a Buddhist Master and Abbot of Gion monastery, who subsequently lived as a hermit until his death.

71. Minamoto no Tsunenobu (1016–1097), a famous poet, musician and Senior Councillor, who, at 80, was appointed governor of the regional Dazaifu government of Kyushu island. Seemingly this was a fate akin to banishment. He died soon after. Late Classical 36.

72. Ki'i (mid–late 11ᵗʰ C), a Lady-in-Waiting to Empress Genshi, a consort to Emperor Go-Suzaku, Lady-in-Waiting to Empress Genshi and subsequently Princess Yushi Naishin'nō, an important literary patron.
NOTE: See poem 42.

73. Masafusa (1041–1111), a child prodigy in Chinese studies who became an important writer in Chinese as well as Japanese. He was a renowned administrator and Acting Middle Counsellor.

74. Minamoto no Toshiyori (1055–1129), a courtier and son of Minamoto no Tsunenobu (poem 71) who was considered the best poet and critic among his contemporaries. In famous debates with Fujiwara no Mototoshi (poem 75) he championed a new poetics.
NOTE: A Bodhisattva is a person on the way to becoming a Buddha. One of the most famous of these is Kannon, the Bodhisattva of mercy and Hatsuseno is the site of the famous Hasedera Temple, associated with her worship.

75. Fujiwara no Mototoshi (1060–1142), a leading poet but considered old fashioned by Minamoto no Toshiyori and his followers. Late Classical 36.
NOTE: See poem 51.

76. Hosshōji Kanpaku or Fujiwara no Tadamichi (1097–1164), a Lay Buddhist Novice and former Chancellor of the Realm. He was father of Jien (poem 95) and a highly regarded poet in Japanese and Chinese.

77. Emperor Sutoku (1119–1164), 75th Emperor of Japan, he instigated a revolt after he was forced to abdicate. Subsequently exiled to Shikoku, he was a respected poet and editor.

78. Minamoto no Kanemasa (early 12th C), part of the famous poetry circle of Emperor Horikawa. This poem was often echoed in later literature.

79. Sakyō no Daibu Akisuke or Fujiwara no Akisuke(1090–1155), the father of Fujiwara no Kiyosuke (poem 84). He was ordered by Emperor Sutoku to compile the Imperial Anthology Shikashū.

80. Horikawa (12th C), a lady in the court of Empress Dowager Taiken. In 1143 they both took religious orders. Late Classical 36.

81. Gotokudaiji (1139–1191), a renowned poet and musician. A nephew of Toshinari (poem 83) and cousin of Fujiwara no Teika (poem 97) he was made Minister of the Left and took religious orders just before his death.

82. Dōin (1090–c.1179), Lieutenant of the Stable of the Left who later took religious orders and became a Buddhist Master.

83. Toshinari or Fujiwara no Shunzei (1114–1204), Private Secretary to the Empress and a leading poet-critic who compiled the 7th Imperial Poetry Anthology. Father to Fujiwara no Teika (poem 97), compiler of the Ogura Hyakunin Isshu.
NOTE: See poem 5.

84. Fujiwara no Kiyosuke (1104–1177), son of Fujiwara no Akisuke (poem 79), he was a courtier, leading poet and scholar whose innovations and standards of judging poetry made him a rival of Fujiwara no Shunzei (poem 83).

85. Shun'e or Tayū no Kimi (1113–c. 1191), a Buddhist Master who produced a private poetry collection, the Rin'yō Wakashū. Late Classical 36.

86. Saigyō (1118 – 1190), a Buddhist Master from his early 20's, he was a good friend of Fujiwara no Teika (poem 97). He is best known for the many long, poetic journeys he took that would later inspire the famous haiku poet, Bashō.

87. Jakuren or Fujiwara no Sadanaga (1139–1202), a well-regarded poet close to Fujiwara no Shunzei (poem 83) and his son Fujiwara no Teika (poem 97). After he became a Buddhist Master, he travelled widely composing poems.

88. Lady-in-Waiting to Empress Dowager Kōka (12th C), real name unknown, daughter of the poet, Minamoto no Toshitaka, her birth and death dates are unknown, but we know she became a nun in 1181.
Note: See poem 19.

89. Princess Shikishi (c. 1149 –1201), may have studied with Fujiwara no Shunzei (poem 83). She was very close to his son Fujiwara no Teika (poem 97) whose diary records her ongoing health struggles and how she become a nun just before her death.

90. Undersecretary to Empress Dowager Inpu (c. 1130–c. 1200), real name unknown, her work appears in a large number of Imperial poetry collections.

NOTE: See also 42. Here, as in poems 42, 65, 72 and 92, overwhelming grief is illustrated by how wet one's sleeves are. This poem takes it to the extreme with tears of blood, a reference to a classical Chinese story. A farmer displeased a king and had his feet cut off as a punishment. He is described as crying so bitterly that his tears dried up and turned to blood.

91. Gokyōgoku Sesshō or Fujiwara no Yoshitsune (1169–1206), child prodigy who became Minister of the Left at 38 but died soon after. He wrote the preface to the Shinkonjakuwakashū. Late Classical 36.

NOTE: Lovers often used each other's kimono sleeves (sode 袖) as pillows. Here the practice of katajiki (片敷き), or having to use one's own kimono sleeves because one is sleeping alone, is introduced. See also 62 and poems 42 and 95 for notes on other sleeve metaphors.

92. Sanuki or Chūgū Sanuki (c. 1141–1217), a poet, member of the Minamoto clan and courtier to Emperor Nijō. Late Classical 36.

NOTE: See poem 42.

93. Minamoto no Sanetomo or Kamakura (1192–1219), third Shōgun of the Kamakura shogunate, supposedly tutored by Fujiwara no Teika (poem 97) who considered him one of the greatest poets of the time. He was assassinated at age 28.

94. Asukai Masatsune (1170–1221), accomplished poet and player of kemari, a classical Japanese form of football. He was an Associate Councillor who served under three Emperors including Emperors Go-Toba (poem 99) and Juntoku (poem 100). Late Classical 36.

95. Ji'en (1155–1225), a Former High Priest, poet and influential historian who rose to become leader of the Tendai order. He was the son of Tadamichi (poem 76) and uncle of Yoshitsune (poem 91). Late Classical 36.

NOTE: In this poem a sleeve metaphor is used to indicate the robes of a Japanese Buddhist monk. For notes on other sleeve metaphors see poem 42 and 67.

96. Saionji Kintsune, a member of the Fujiwara clan, he was a former Chancellor of the Realm who became a Lay Buddhist Novice. He was a brother in law of Fujiwara no Teika (poem 97).

97. Fujiwara no Teika (1162–1241) or **Sadaie**, son of **Fujiwara no Shunzei** (poem 83), considered among the greatest of Japanese poets (in particular of the waka or tanka form). Influential as a critic and editor, he compiled the Ogura Hyakunin Isshu as well as Imperial Anthologies and other classic texts. He was an Acting Middle Councillor.

NOTE: One of the earliest salt-making methods in Japan involved burning seaweed and using the resultant ashes. Later, boiled seawater was also used in the production of moshio (藻塩) or seaweed salt.

98. Fujiwara no Ietaka (1158–1237), or **Jūni no Ietaka**, a son in law of Jakuren (poem 87) and pupil of Fujiwara no Shunzei (poem 83). As Director of Palace Affairs, he was close to Emperor Go-Toba (poem 99).

99. Emperor Go-Toba (1180–1239), 82nd Emperor of Japan, who abdicated at 18 and was later exiled to the Oki Islands. Father of Emperor Juntoku (poem 100), friend and patron to Fujiwara no Teika (poem 97) he developed as a calligrapher, musician, poet, and editor.

100. Emperor Juntoku (1197–1242), 84th Emperor of Japan and son of Emperor Go-Toba (poem 99). He studied under Fujiwara no Teika (poem 97) and left a large body of writings. He was exiled to Sado Island in 1221.

Sources include Peter MacMillan's *100 Poets, One Poem Each,* Kenneth Rexroth's *One Hundred Poems from the Japanese,* as well as various online sources including the Ogurasansō (https://www.ogurasansou.co.jp/site/hyakunin/index.html).

The Translators

James Hadley is Ussher Assistant Professor in Literary Translation at Trinity College Dublin. He is the Director of the College's master's degree in Literary Translation, which is based at the Trinity Centre for Literary and Cultural Translation. After studying Japanese and Computing at the undergraduate level and later Buddhism and Translation Studies at the master's level, James completed a PhD in Translation Studies in 2013. Since then, James has become known as one of the leading theoretical researchers in indirect translation, or the translation of translations. James is a strong proponent of using computer-based tools in the production of translation research. James is also very interested in practices that stretch our casual assumptions about what translation is and how it functions.

Nell Regan is a poet and non-fiction writer based in Dublin. She has published three collections of poetry; *Preparing for Spring, Bound for Home* (both Arlen House, 2007, 2011) and *One Still Thing* (Enitharmon Press, 2014). Awards include an Arts Council Literature Bursary, a Fellowship at the International Writing Programme, Iowa and she has been a Fulbright Scholar at U.C Berkeley as well as a Patrick and Katherine Kavanagh Fellow. Her biography *Helena Molony, A Radical Life, 1883–1967* (Arlen House,

2017) was an Irish Independent 2017 Book of the Year. Her translations of the Irish language poetry of Micheál Mac Liammóir have been published in *Poetry Ireland Review* and *Cyphers*. She works freelance as an educator and literary programmer.

See also *www.nellregan.com*.

**DEDALUS
PRESS**

*"One of the most outward-looking
poetry presses in Ireland and the UK"*
—UNESCO.org

Named for James Joyce's literary alter ego,
Dedalus Press is one of Ireland's longest running
and best-known literary imprints, dedicated to
contemporary Irish poetry, and to poetry
from around the world in English translation.

For more information, or to purchase copies
of this or other Dedalus Press titles,
please visit us at *www.dedaluspress.com*.

*Poetry Matters:
Spread the Word*